Did you know that some maps can tell time? Some show the weather in Kenya while others show the kinds of plants that grow in Sri Lanka. In this book you'll become familiar with many types of maps. So gather your supplies and get ready.

Note to Parents

For each type of map presented, there are activities and questions that reinforce the essential skills related to that map type. The format of the text proceeds from simple to more complex. Although this book is designed for grades 4-6, it may be used by children younger or older, depending on motivation, maturity, and prior experience.

The following tools will be needed to to do the activities:

- rulers (inches and centimeters)
- colored pencils
- string

Other types of geographic reference materials will be helpful:

- an atlas
- a world globe

In this book, we will be exploring many different kinds of maps. Here are some of the major types of maps that we will use:

Political maps show...   (see page 4)

- Boundaries between countries, states, counties
- Capitals and other cities
- The basic shape and size of the countries

Physical maps show...   (see page 8)

- What the land looks like
- Terrain features such as:

  mountain ranges

  plains

  rivers and lakes

  elevations

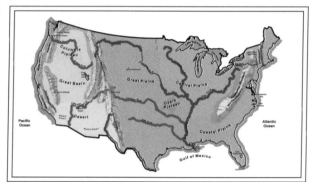

Symbol maps can show...   (see page 6)

- Population
- Crops produced
- Products manufactured
- Many other things

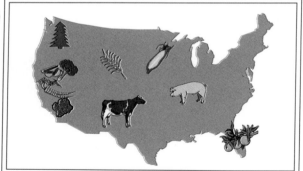

Comparison maps can show... (see page 10)

- differences in location
- differences utilizing scale
- differences using symbols

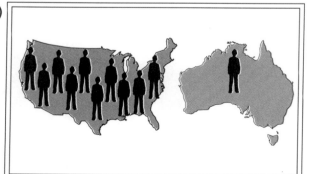

4142

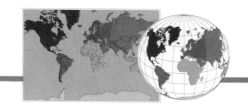

Weather maps show...   (see page 12)

    • Major weather situations

      using symbols

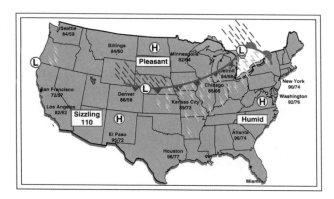

Isometric maps show...   (see page 14)

    • Weather information such as:

      air pressure

      temperatures

      amount of rainfall

      cloud cover

    • Areas of equal elevation

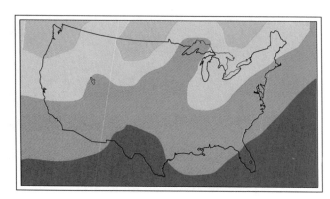

Road maps show...   (see page 16)

    • Highways and roads

    • Cities and towns

    • Places of interest such as:

      national parks

      historic places

    • Distance charts

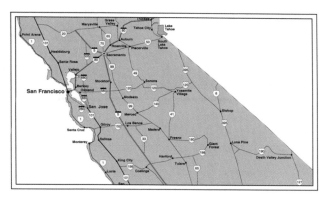

Imaginary line maps show... see page 20)

    • Latitude and longitude

    • Time zones

    • Tilt of the earth as related

      to the sun

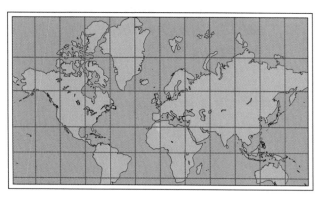

Here is a political map of Southeast Asia. Study it and the legend at the bottom which explains what the map symbols mean. A scale is also provided to help you understand distances on the map.

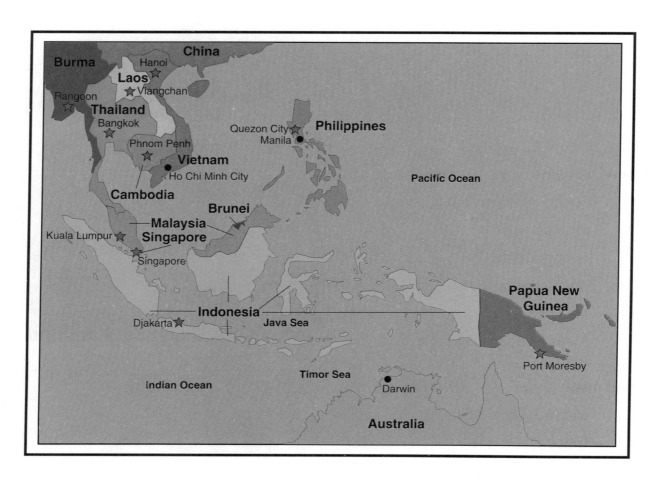

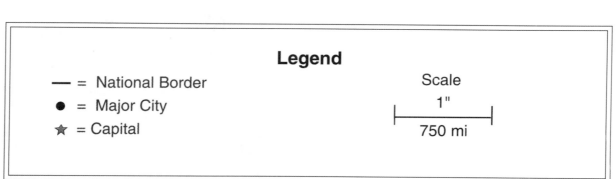

Legend

— = National Border

● = Major City

★ = Capital

Scale

1"

750 mi

Interpreting a Political Map

A political map shows political boundaries, or borders, which separate one government from another. Major cities and bodies of water may also be included on a political map.

How many countries can you find on the map on page 4? _____

Which is the larger, Thailand or Cambodia? _____.

Use a ruler to measure from Singapore to Rangoon. How many inches? _____

Multiply this by the number of miles per inch. How far is it in miles? _____

Draw the symbol used to show major cities:

Three major cities are shown that are not capitals. Which three cities are they?

_____   _____

_____

Which Southeast Asian capital is farthest east? _____

west? _____ south? _____ north? _____

ACTIVITIES:

1. Compare the size of this region with your own country.

2. Find out what kind of government each country shown on this map has.

3. One country, Thailand, has never been a colony of another country. What countries once ruled other Southeast Asian lands? What made these European countries give up their colonies? Use an encyclopedia or computer program to find out.

4. Which Southeast Asian country would you most like to visit? Give several reasons and illustrate a typical scene from this country.

A symbol is something that represents another thing. Maps use symbols because they are easier than drawing real-looking objects. Sometimes symbols look like the thing they represent. This is a symbol of a bridge >—< . Sometime symbols do not look like the thing they represent. This is a symbol for a steelmill $\boxed{S}$. Study the map below to see how symbols are used.

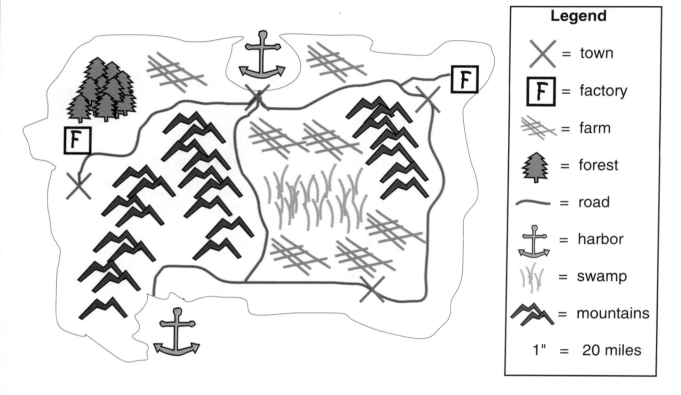

1. How many towns are shown?_____ All of the towns are connected by _____.

2. There are three distinct natural land features on the island. They are:

   _____, _____, _____.

3. The one natural feature that takes up the most of the land area is _____

4. Which town do you think would be the best one to live in? Why? _____

   _____

5. Two harbors are shown on the island. Which one do you think would be the better

   one and why? _____

4142

Making a Symbol Map

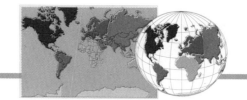

Now you have a chance to show how clever you can be with map symbols. Draw a map below and devise a system of symbols to represent real things. Make sure to include as many details as you can to make it interesting and fun to look at. Make sure your legend explains each symbol used.

Let's make this a map of a city. If you feel that you can, you could make it a map of the city where you live, or of a real city nearby. If you make a symbol map of an imaginary city, give it a name.

This is a symbol map of: _____

Legend

Symbols:

    = _____

    = _____

    = _____

    = _____

    = _____

    = _____

Scale:

1" = _____ mi.

What symbol could you use for buildings, parks, homes, streets, highways, etc.?

Physical Maps

Physical maps attempt to show what the land looks like. They show land and water forms. Often cities and borders are added to create a combination map.

Here is a pure physical map showing landforms:

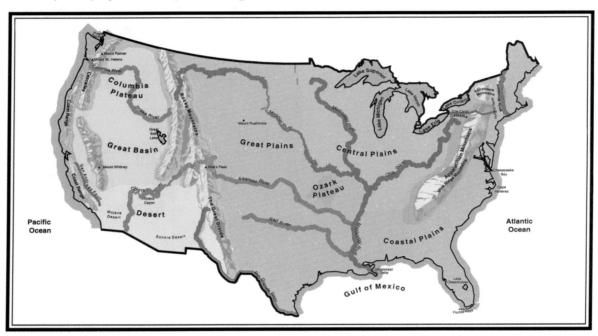

Here is what a combination map looks like:

4142

Make a Physical Map

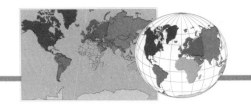

Here is an imaginary place. Your job is to draw in its physical features, such as mountains, rivers, lakes, and oceans. Use colored pencils or crayons to make the region look as real as possible. Before you start, fill in the legend box to show scale and any other symbols you plan to use.

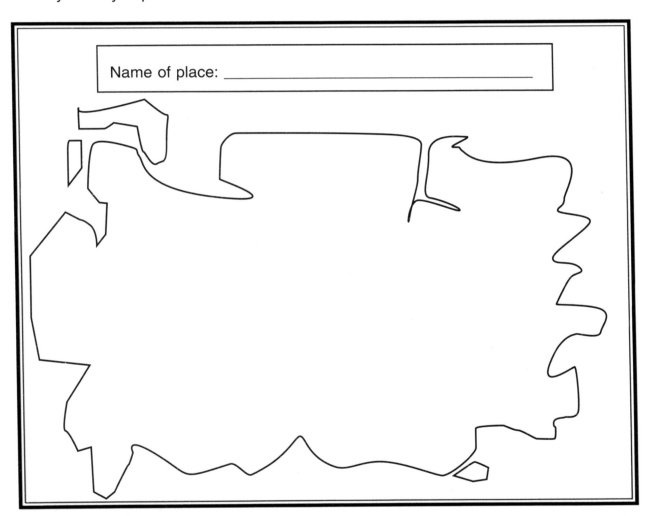

Name of place: _____

LEGEND

Symbols:

= _____   = _____   Scale:

= _____   = _____   1" = _____ miles

= _____   = _____

The maps below use symbols, colored zones, or dots to make a comparison. Study them.

Map 1

Population Comparison using numbers of symbols

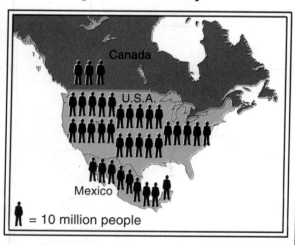

Canada

U.S.A.

Mexico

= 10 million people

Map 2

Rainfall Comparison using colored or shaded zones

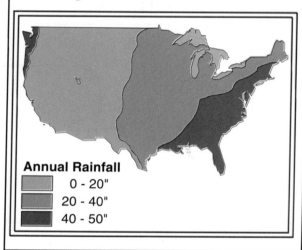

Annual Rainfall

0 - 20"

20 - 40"

40 - 50"

Map 3

Density Comparison using dots

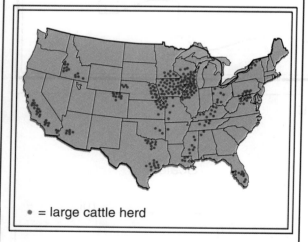

• = large cattle herd

Map 4

Energy Use Comparison using sizes of a symbol

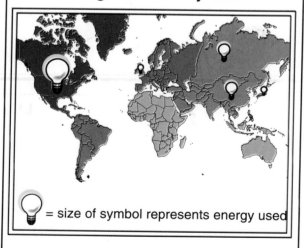

= size of symbol represents energy used

Interpreting Comparison Maps

Use the maps on page 10 to answer these questions, use the map on page 8 to locate state names.

MAP I: 1.   One symbol = how many people? _____

              2.   Which country has the most people? _____

              3.   Which country has the fewest people? _____

              4.   How many people live in the U.S.A.? _____

              5.   How many people live in Mexico? _____

MAP 2:   1.   How much rain does coastal Oregon get? _____

              2.   How much rain do Great Lakes states get? _____

              3.   Which side of Texas gets 20-40" of rain? _____

              4.   Except for the Pacific Northwest,
the climate gets _____ as you go west. _____

MAP 3:   1.   Which state looks full of cattle? _____

              2.   Which northwest state has many cattle? _____

              3.   Which southwest state has many cattle? _____

              4.   Which part of Florida has more cattle? _____

              5.   What area of the U.S. has the most cattle? _____

MAP 4: You will need a map of the world. Of the countries with energy use identified:

              1.   Which country uses the most energy? _____

               2.   Which country uses the least energy? _____

               3.   Which two countries use about the same? _____

The map below is much like the one shown every day in your newspaper. It uses symbols to explain what the weather is going to be for a certain date. This map shows a typical summer day in the United States.

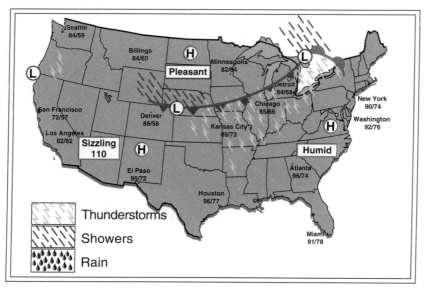

Weather moves in fairly large masses of air. Wet weather is characterized by low pressure. Areas of high pressure are usually dry. On a weather map, a letter **L** means low pressure; a letter **H** means high pressure.

Meteorologists use instruments called barometers to tell what the air pressure is. Using these devices, they can predict what the weather.

The borders between areas of high and low pressure are called fronts. The diagram below shows symbols that are used to show fronts on a weather map. The side of the front line that has the points or bumps on it tells the direction the front is moving.

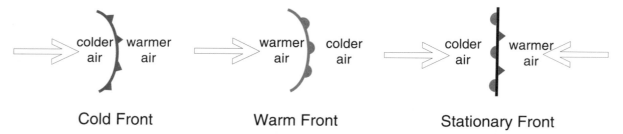

The weather on one side of a front is usually different from the weather on the other side.. Look at the weather map at the top of this page. Notice how the temperatures and weather are different on the sides of the major front that runs across the center of the country.

The weather map shows what the temperatures are around the nation. In this case the temperatures are shown in Fahrenheit degrees. A weather map in Europe would use Celsius degrees.

Interpreting Weather Maps

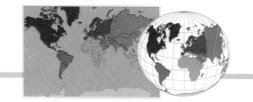

Use the weather map on page 12 to answer these questions:

1. This weather map shows that North Dakota, New Mexico, and Virginia have
   _____ pressure. How would you describe the weather in those three places?
   _____.

2. The most common precipitation symbol shown on the map for this day is _____
   _____.

   What air pressure symbol do you notice being close to these?_____

3. Two states are having showers. Which ones?
   _____   _____

4. Look up the word "humid" in a dictionary. What does it mean?_____
   _____.

5. List two states having humid weather: _____   _____.

6. Which area of the country has most of the temperatures over 90° — North, South,
   East, or West? _____   .

7. What kind of front stretches between upper Michigan and New York?
   _____

8. What kind of front stretches from Colorado to Chicago? _____

9. What weather do you predict for Chicago for the next day? _____
   _____

10. What is your prediction for Washington D.C.? _____
    _____

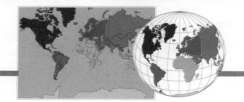

"Iso" means "same" in Greek and "meter" means "measure," so "isometric" means "same measure." These maps are called isometric maps because the lines connect areas of the same elevation, the same temperature, or the the same air pressure.

Topographic Map (the lines on this map are called "isometric" lines)

Temperature Map (the lines on this map are called "isotherms")

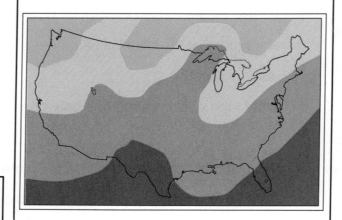

Atmospheric Pressure Map (the lines on this map are called "isobars")

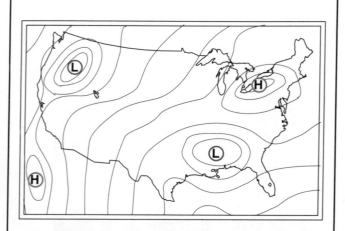

4142

Interpreting Isometric Maps

The pictures below illustrate two ways to show changes in elevation. In the first picture, imagine that you are flying in toward the land in an airplane. In the second illustration, imagine that you are directly above the same area, looking straight down. Notice how the cliff, mountain, and flat valley are shown. Each of the isometric lines in the second illustration represent a 20-foot difference in elevation.

"Topographic" maps like these usually show a fairly small area. They are used most often by hikers, geologists, forest rangers, and city planners. The wavy lines, called contour lines, show elevation, the number of feet, or meters above sea level. When the lines are close together it means that the land is very steep. When they are far apart, it is fairly flat.

On a contour map, you will usually see that roads and trails run along the valley floors where the going is easier. When mountains are shown on contour maps, hikers can tell which routes to the top can be taken by walking, and which would have to be climbed.

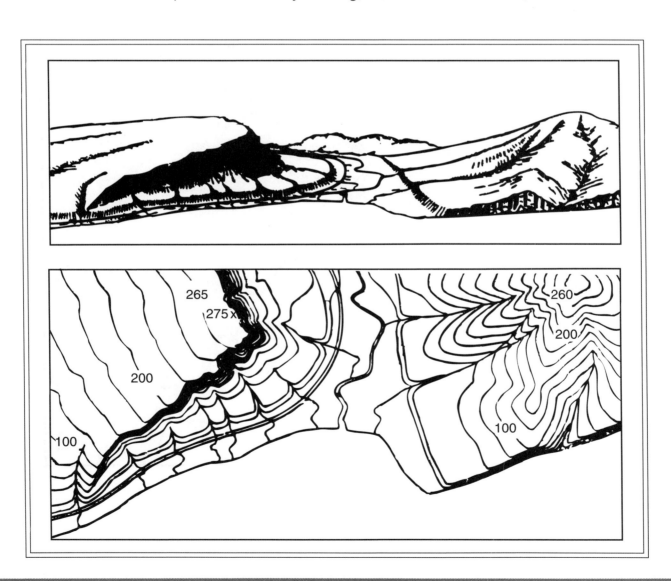

Road maps are designed to show you how to get from one place to another. Imagine that you are up in the sky, able to look straight down on the land below.

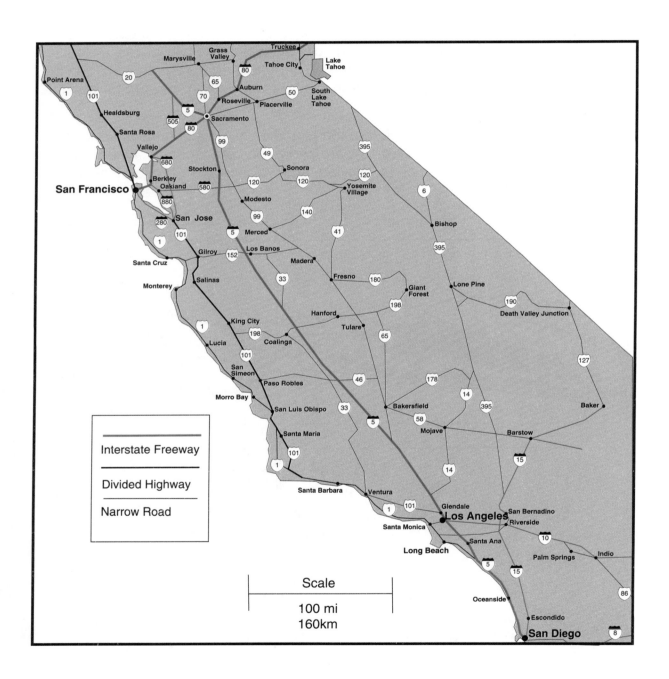

4142

Interpreting Road Maps

Use the road map on page 16 to answer these questions:

1. Approximately how far is it from San Francisco to Los Angeles? _____ mi _____ km.

2. There are three ways you might chose to make a trip from San Francisco to Los Angeles.

    a. If you wanted the scenic, coastal route, you would take Highway _____.

    b. If you took a divided highway for a faster trip, you would take Highway _____.

    c. The interstate freeway that goes down to Los Angeles is Highway _____.

3. If you wanted to go on to San Diego after arriving in Los Angeles, about how much farther would you have to go? _____ mi _____ km.

4. About how far is it from San Francisco to Lake Tahoe? _____ mi _____ km.

5. What interstate freeway connects San Francisco to Lake Tahoe? Highway _____.

6. If you want a more direct route from Sacramento to the Lake, take Highway _____.

7. Why might you choose to take the longer route, using Highway 80?

    _____

    _____ .

Measuring Distances on Maps

Every map is a reduced representation of part of the Earth's surface. Maps come in different sizes, therefore distances on maps vary. Maps are drawn to different scales.

The scale on a map is usually shown as a small ruler at the bottom of the map. By using the scale, you can approximate the actual distances from place to place on the map.

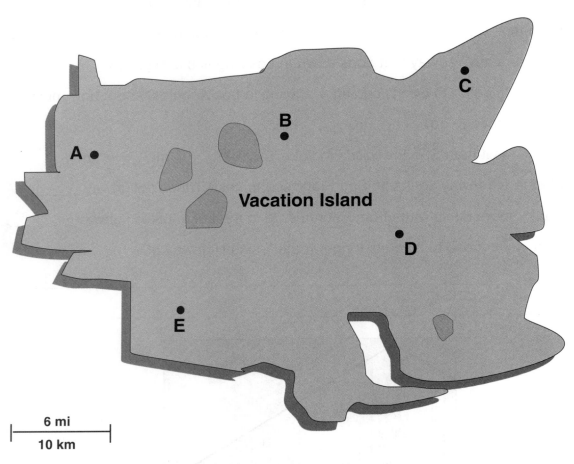

Vacation Island

| 6 mi |
| 10 km |

1. About how far is it from point A to point B on the map above? _____ miles

2. How far is it from B to C? _____ miles

3. How far from C to D? _____ miles

4. How far is it from D to E? _____ miles

5. Now, let's make a round trip.
   About how far is an A - B - C - D - E - A trip on this map? _____ miles

4142

Using a Scale Ruler

Sometimes, rather than providing a scale, a map might come with a special ruler for measuring distances on the map. Such a ruler will only work on that particular map or another map that is drawn to exactly the same scale.

Cut out the two rulers that are on the inside back cover of this book. One gives you distances in miles. The other measures on this map in kilometers.

Measure and record the approximate straight-line distance between the cities below with both rulers:

Boise to Minneapolis _____ mi _____ km

Dallas to Chicago _____ mi _____ km

San Francisco to Miami _____ mi _____ km

St. Louis to Charlotte _____ mi _____ km

Miami to New Orleans _____ mi _____ km

Charlotte to Albuquerque _____ mi _____ km

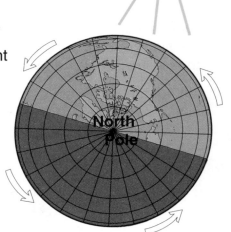

The Earth rotates, causing the sun to rise and set at different times depending on where you are. Because the Earth rotates to the east, the sun comes up in New York before it does in Los Angeles because New York is farther east.

The Earth has been divided into 24 time zones. The time in each zone is one hour earlier than the zone to its east.

When it is noon in New York, it is 11:00 A.M in Chicago, 10:00 A.M. in Denver, and 9:00 A.M. in Los Angeles.

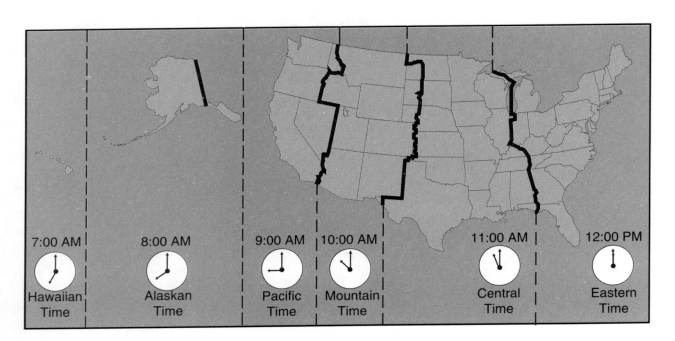

7:00 AM	8:00 AM	9:00 AM	10:00 AM	11:00 AM	12:00 PM
Hawaiian Time	Alaskan Time	Pacific Time	Mountain Time	Central Time	Eastern Time

1. Name the six time zones that stretch from Hawaii to Maine:

   _____, _____, _____,
   _____, _____, _____.

2. If it is 3:00 P.M. in Houston, TX, what time is it in Anchorage, AK?
   _____.

3. A trip from South Bend, IN, to Chicago, IL, takes about two hours. If I left South Bend at 12:00 noon, what time would it be in Chicago when I arrived there:_____.

Notice that the time zone boundary lines aren't perfectly straight. The boundary lines go around heavily populated areas so that people won't have to reset their watches every time they drive across town.

4142

What Time Is It?

Here is a map that shows time zones all around the world. This map doesn't show the wiggles in the actual boundaries. You can see that the Earth is divided into 24 time zones. Each zone is about 15° wide.

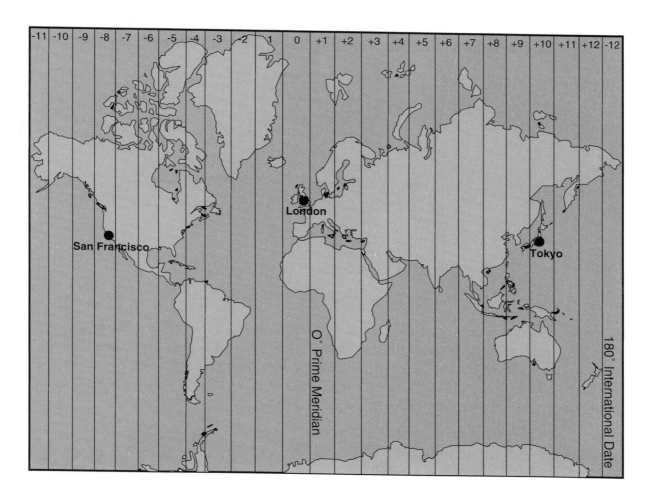

1. In which direction does the time get later?_____

2. How many hours difference from one zone to the next? _____

3. How many hours difference between San Francisco and London? _____

4. In which of those two cities is it later? _____

5. How many hours difference between Tokyo and London?_____

6. If it is 8:00 P.M. in Tokyo, what time is it in London? _____

Even Imaginary Lines Can Be Helpful

How do people describe their location when they are in an ocean or in a remote area where there are no city names or other landmarks? Early mapmakers decided to begin with two imaginary lines. One of them connects the North Pole to the South Pole. We call that the **prime meridian**. The other runs all the way around the Earth, always midway between the two poles. We call that line the **equator**. All map directions start with these two crossed lines. We use more imaginary lines to tell exactly what our global address is.

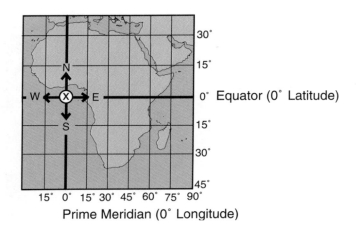

When we tell directions on a map, we always tell how far north or south we are first. Then we say how far east or west. Let's pretend the Earth is a huge spherical building. We have to enter where the equator and the Prime Meridian cross (0º,0º). From there we can take an imaginary elevator that always goes north or south. Then we step off and take imaginary moving sidewalks to the east or west.

There are 90 floors (actually, degrees of latitude) going north and 90 floors going south. Floor zero is the equator. The North Pole is floor 90 north (geographers would say 90° N). The South Pole is floor 90 south, or 90° south.

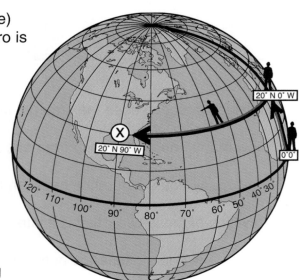

Once we reach the floor we want, we can go either east or west to the exact global "address" (degrees of longitude) we want to find. Let's say we want to visit New Orleans, Louisiana. The global address 20° north and 90° west. We start at 0°,0° or where the equator and prime meridian cross. We ride the elevator to the south to the 33rd floor and get out. Then we hop on the moving sidewalk going west to the address we want, 90° west. We made it!

On a globe, use your finger to trace the same trip.

4142

Using Map Coordinates

Let's practice using the two maps below.

Latitude   means distance in degrees north or south of the equator.

Longitude   means distance east or west of the prime meridian.

The position of the letter **A** is:

__30__ ° __N__ latitude, __30__ ° __W__ longitude.

1. What is the position of the letter **B**?

_____ ° ____ latitude, _____ ° ____ longitude

2. What is the position of the letter **C**?

_____ ° ____ latitude, _____ ° ____ longitude.

3. Draw a heavy **dot** at the following position:

__15__ ° __S__ latitude, __45__ ° __E__ longitude.

Map of Africa:

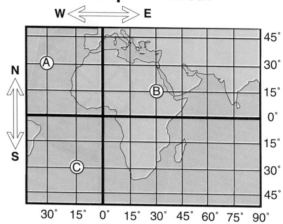

The position of the letter **D** is:

__30__ ° __S__ latitude, __90__ ° __W__ longitude.

1. What is the position of the letter **E**?

_____ ° ____ latitude, _____ ° ____ longitude

2. What is the position of the letter **F**?

_____ ° ____ latitude, _____ ° ____ longitude.

3. Draw a ● at the following position:

__0__ º latitude, __60__ º __W__ longitude.

Map of South America:

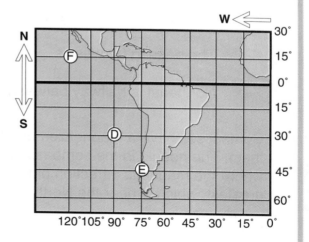

People have been finding their way with compasses for centuries. These magical instruments with their magnetic arrows guided Columbus and Magellan to discover the "new" world. They can help you, too. Let's look at one and see how it is organized.

First, look at the four main directions: north, south, east, and west. Labeling just those four basic directions is too limiting when you want to give directions. You can see how the "in between" directions are named.

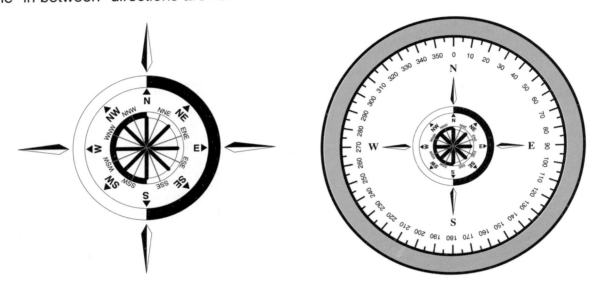

Notice the ring of numbers surrounding the directional words. These numbers are more exact than directions in word form. They tell precisely which direction a compass needle is pointing. North is the starting point and is always called 0°. You can see that East is shown as 90°. Directions in number form or degrees are called "bearings."

The bearing pointing south is _____°.

The bearing for west is _____°.

Northeast is halfway between 0° and 90°, so it is_____°.

Compasses have a magnetized needle in them. The needle in the compass points to where the magnetic attraction of the Earth is greatest, which is near the North Pole.

If you hold a compass and turn it so that the **N** is under the point of the needle, the compass then shows you all the other directions and bearings.

Using a Compass

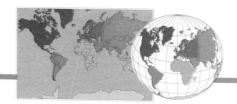

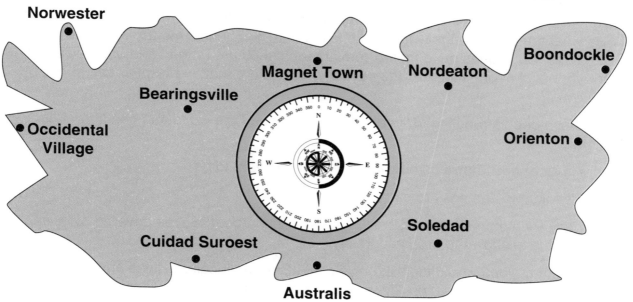

Norwester

Magnet Town

Nordeaton

Boondockle

Bearingsville

Occidental Village

Orienton

Cuidad Suroest

Soledad

Australis

Let's practice with compass directions and bearings using the map above.

On the map above, we have placed a compass right on top of Centerville, where you are. Your job is to complete the chart below, telling both the direction and the bearing you would travel to get to each town. Use abbreviations for the directions. Make sure to put the degree symbol (°) to the upper right of all bearings.

TOWN	DIRECTION	BEARING
MAGNET TOWN	_____	_____
OCCIDENTAL VILLAGE	_____	_____
ORIENTON	_____	_____
SOLEDAD	_____	_____
BEARINGSVILLE	_____	_____
NORWESTER	_____	_____
BOONDOCKLE	_____	_____
NORDEATON	_____	_____
AUSTRALIS	_____	_____
CUIDAD SUROESTE	_____	_____

As you know, the Earth is a spherical planet. Therefore, the only way to make a map that shows what the planet actually looks like is to make a spherical model. This is why we have globes. But globes have their disadvantages: they are hard to fold up; they are too big for your pocket or backpack; they usually show more than we want to see at one time.

People have been struggling for years to make maps of the world that can show it in a way that:

- is clear and shows us how to get where we want to go.

- is foldable and easy to carry.

This is easy for a map showing a small area, but the larger the area covered by a map, the harder it is to show the area accurately.

Imagine what a globe would look like if you cut along the longitude lines and stretched it out flat. It would look something like an orange peel that has been cut and spread out on a flat surface.

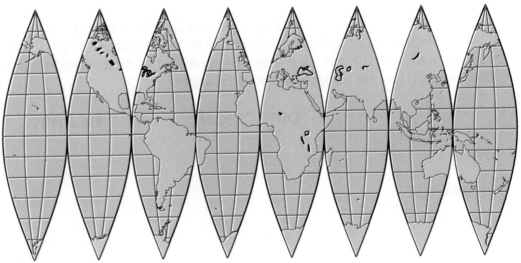

Mapmakers found those spaces between the points that were the north and south poles annoying, so they just stretched them. This flat map of the earth, is called the *Mercator projection*, after its inventor.

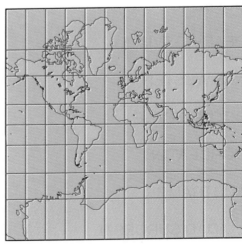

4142

Let's compare a globe and the Mercator projection on page 26. You need to have a real globe to use. On the globe, use a piece of string to measure the width (east to west) of the United States.

On your globe, the U.S. is _____ inches wide.

Now measure the length (north to south) of the United States on the globe

On your globe, the U.S. is _____ inches high.

Make the same measurements with Greenland. It is _____ " wide and _____ " high.

Use the Mercator projection on page 26 (or a bigger one if you have one). On that map:

The United States is _____ inches wide.   Greenland is _____ inches wide.

The United States is _____ inches high.   Greenland is _____ inches high.

Can you see that Greenland looks much bigger on the Mercator projection? The closer to the poles you get, the more distortion there is. On a globe, the vertical lines all come together at the poles. On a Mercator projection, the vertical lines are as far apart at the poles as they are at the equator. This makes it possible to show the Earth on a flat map, but it changes comparative sizes.

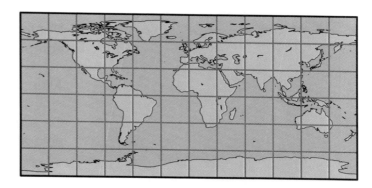

What do you think would be a solution for the distortion caused by Mercator's projection? Did you think of something like the figure below? This is called a Robinson projection. No flat map can accurately show the ball-shaped Earth, but this is another way to try.

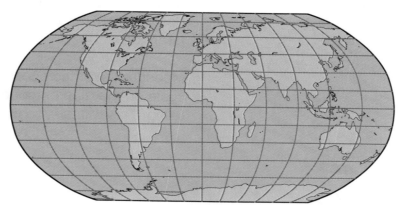

The activities on this page will require a globe, a flat map of the world, string (24"), a ruler, and a compass you can cut out from the inside back cover. The bigger the map and globe, the better.

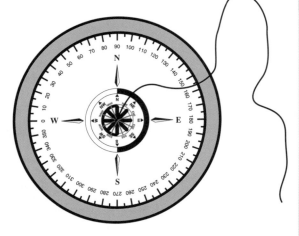

- Punch a tiny hole in the center of your compass.

- Run a string with a knot in the end through the hole. The knot should end up beneath the compass, with the loose end of the string sticking out from the top.

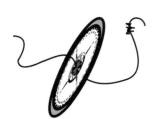

Now you have a fabulous, reusable map tool. Here is how to use it to find out the direction and distance to a location on a map or globe:

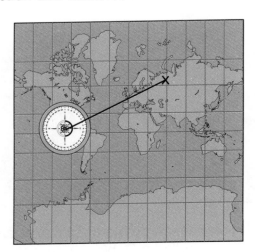

- Put the very center of your compass over your starting point.

- Align the north arrow directly north.

- On a globe, point it toward the north pole at the top of the globe.

- On a flat map, point it straight up toward the top of the map, directly above its position.

- Stretch the string directly to your destination. This will tell you the bearing.

- Measure the string according to the scale on the map or globe you are using. This will tell you the distance.

4142

Comparing Maps and Globes

Let's use our paper compass and string to determine the bearing (direction) and the distance for a trip from San Francisco, California, U.S.A. to Moscow, Russia.

First, use the compass to make the measurements on a flat map. The scale **on the map** will help you determine the distance. Notice the places the string passes over as you measure. Those would be the places you would see out of your airplane window.

Flat map answers:

Bearing from San Francisco to Moscow: _____

Distance from San Francisco to Moscow: _____

Now, use your compass to make the same measurements on a globe. Take the shortest route. Use the scale **on the globe** to determine the distance. Again, notice the places the string passes over.

Globe answers:

Bearing from San Francisco to Moscow: _____

Distance from San Francisco to Moscow: _____

Did the string pass over the same places when you measured on the map and globe?

Did the distances come out the same with both measurements?

Did the bearings come out the same with both measurements?

Which do you think gives you a more accurate bearing, a map or a globe?

What makes the difference in the answers?

Now you know why ships and planes need navigators. For every trip, you need a trained person and accurate tools to know which direction to go and how much fuel you will need to get there. And, even if you have planned your trip carefully, weather or other conditions might cause you to take a different route. When your plane goes around a storm or is blown off course by the wind, the navigator has to make new calculations to get you to your destination.

Distance Chart

Maps and travel brochures often show distances between cities on a chart similar to the one below. See if you can fill in the empty blanks on the distance chart by writing the mileage that you measured from page 19. The distance between Boise and Minneapolis has been filled in to show you how. For more practice, you can do the mesurements and fill in the shaded areas, too.

	San Francisco	Boise	Minneapolis	Chicago	St. Louis	Charlotte	Miami	New Orleans	Dallas	Albuquerque
San Francisco	X									
Boise		X	1225 mi 1890 km							
Minneapolis		1225 mi 1890 km	X							
Chicago				X						
St. Louis					X					
Charlotte						X				
Miami							X			
New Orleans								X		
Dallas									X	
Albuquerque										X

4142

Geographic Resources

One of the best sources for many types of maps is the United States Geological Survey. The two main offices are in Washington, D.C. 20242 and Denver, CO 80225. They will send you a free catalog of the types of maps they sell, along with ordering instructions. The prices are very low.

Computers are wonderful geographic tools. Many programs exist that will provide almost limitless possibilities for geographic applications. Some recommended programs are:

• *Mac Globe* and *PC Globe* both provide a computerized atlas, along with an array of statistical information on all countries. Flags, national anthems, economic facts, and cultural/physical statistics are all included. Order through Broderbund Software.

• National Geographic Society's *ZipZapMap* geographic game provides geographic concepts in an enjoyable format.

• Also from National Geographic Society is the *Picture Atlas of the World*, a CD-ROM program in an interactive format.

• World Wide Web on the Internet offers information on countries and cultures served by the Peace Corps. *World Wise Schools* study guides are also available. Call the Peace Corps Office of World Wise Schools at (202)606-3294 or (800)424-8580, ext 2283, for the site address.

Also, look for these other geography books in this *Learning Horizons* series:
  • *United States Geography*
  • *World Geography*
  • *Cultures Around the World*

Canada and the United States have a Geograpic Alliance Network. A list is available from Cynthia Jacobs-Carter, D.C. Geographic Alliance, 2020 Pennsylvania Ave. Suite 300, Washington D.C. 20006

Global Geography: Activities for Teaching the Five Themes of Geography, Social Science Education Consortium, Boulder, Colorado, grade 3 - 9, (303)492-8154.

For a free catalog of cultural awareness publications, call the Center for Teaching International Relations (CTR), University of Denver, at 1 (800)967-2847. Examples of publications:
  • Global partner: Skills for a Changing World, grades K-8
  • Passport to Understanding, grades K-6
  • Teaching About Cultural Awareness, grades 5-12

Answers

Page 5

12 countries
Thailand
2 inches
1500 miles
major cities: dots
   Ho Chi Minh City
   Manila
   Kuala Lumpur
east: Port Moresby
west: Rangoon
south: Port Moresby
north: Hanoi

Page 6

1. 4, roads
2. forest, mountains, swamp.
3. mountains
4. Answers will vary.
5. Answers will vary.

Page 11

Map 1 1. 10,000,000
        2. U.S.A.
        3. Canada
        4. 250,000,000
        5. 90,000,000
Map 2 1. 40 - 50 "
        2. 20 - 40 "
        3. east
        4. drier
Map 3 1. Iowa
        2. Idaho
        3. Arizona
        4. southern
        5. mid-west
Map 4 1. U.S.A.
        2. United Kingdom (Great Britain)
        3. China and Russia

Page 12

1. hot
2. thunderstorms, low
3. Wyoming, Nebraska
4. damp or moist
5. North Carolina, South Carolina
6. south
7. warm front
8. cold front
9. rain
10. continued hot weather

Page 13

1. high warm, dry, sunny
2. rain, low
3. Wyoming, Nebraska
4. moist, high water content in the air
5. New Mexico, Virginia
6. Southeast, Southwest
7. warm front
8. cold front
9. clear and warmer
10. thunderstorms

Page 17

1. 325 mi, 500 km
2. a. 1
   b. 101
   c. 5
3. 100 mi, 160 km
4. 150 mi, 240 km
5. 80
6. 50
7. A freeway is wider and faster than a narrow mountain road.

Page 18

1. A - B 10 mi   18 km
2. B - C 12 mi   20 km
3. C - D   9 mi   15 km
4. D - E 14 mi   22 km
5. A----A 57 mi   95 km

Page 19

Will vary a little using rulers:
B - M   1225 mi 1890 km
D - Ch   900 mi 1375 km
SF - M 2800 mi 4375 km
S L-Ch   640 mi 1000 km
M - NO   700 mi 1125 km
Ch - Al 1600 mi 2520 km

Page 20

1. Hawaiian, Alaskan, Pacific, Mountain, Central, Eastern
2. 12:00 noon
3. 1:00 pm

Page 21

1. later toward the east
2. one hour between zones
3. 8 hours difference
4. London is later
5. 10 hours difference
6. 10:00 am in London

Page 23

B   15º N lat   30º E long
C   30º S lat   15º W long

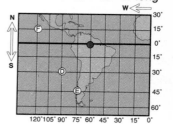

E   45° S lat   75° W long
F   15° N lat 120° W long

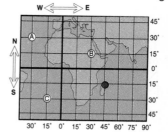

Page 24

South is 180°
West is 270°
Northeast is 45°

Page 25

Magnet Town	N	0°
Occident. Village	W	270°
Orienton	E	90°
Soledad	SE	135°
Bearingsville	WNW	295°
Norwester	NW	320°
Boondockle	ENE	60°
Nordeaton	NE	45°
Australis	S	180º
Cuidad Suroeste	SW	225°

Page 29

Measurements will vary with the map or globes you use, but there will be a big difference between the bearing you get with any flat map compared to any globe. Seeing what the string passes over will make you notice that the flight from San Francisco to Moscow takes what is often called "the polar route." Your plane would go up and over the top side of the world to get to Moscow. A flat map is distorted, so it looks like you would fly across the U. S. to get there. The globe is more accurate because it is shaped like the real Earth.

Page 30

The answers will be the same as on page 19, but shown in a different way.